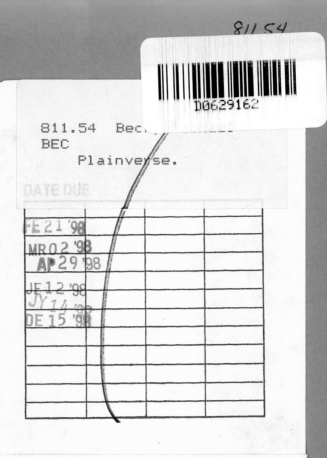

PLAINVERSE
For People Who Can't Stand Obscure Poetry

by Rachael Beck
illustrations by Ann Timberman

GUILDCRAFT of INDIANA
A DIVISION of GUILD PRESS
6000 SUNSET LANE INDIANAPOLIS, IN 46208

ISBN: 1878208-11-X

Additional Timberman sketches
lent by Patti Valentine, Barry Patrick,
Margot Faught and Young Audiences of Indiana.

The "Wrong Line" appeared in *Light Year 1988-89*

A word about Rachael—and Ann...

I was born and grew up in Indianapolis. I have lived elsewhere but keep returning. I've been writing free verse for about fifteen years: observations, truisms, feelings that reflect my career as housewife, mother, grandmother, community volunteer. I am blessed to have a remarkable family, remarkable friends, and the gift of an inborn sense of humor.

Some years ago I asked Ann Timberman to illustrate verses for a book. She responded with nine pictures that are in this volume. To augment Ann's pen-and-ink drawings, I've added casual sketches she'd given me. Two other illustrations and assorted fragments have been borrowed from friends.

My first experience with Ann Timberman's pen and ink illustrations came when she worked a brief stint at the Indiana Arts Commission in 1980. When Ann read my homemade xeroxed pamphlet of verses, she quickly drew a handsome tree of life for the cover of my *Occupation: Housewife.* That was the start of a friendship and working relationship in the field of arts-in-education. Skilled teacher and artist, Ann was also a champion golfer who played occasional rounds with non-champion me. It was during those excursions that I learned that within her witty, charming personality was a modest, shy, sensitive woman dealing with the problems that life dumps on all of us from time to time. Ann could draw them; I scribbled about them.

Tragically, on January 30, 1991, Ann died of cancer, as did my husband, Sigmund Beck, on June 27, 1991. We had enjoyed a number of golf threesomes, Ann the champ, I the "non," and in the middle Sig, the competitive athlete.

Rachael Beck   1991

Endless thanks to "my group" of one-to-one
consultants who offered pointed and intelligent
advice, then generously allowed me to take it or leave it...

VERSES HEREIN

INDOORS AND OUT

COMMON GROUND

For Sig and Ann, in memory of
pleasant twilight threesomes

INDOORS AND OUT

JUST ASKING

Do you ever
go to the post-office for stamps
but leave at home the letters
you need to mail?
Do you ever
take three garments to the cleaners
but forget the one
you want to wear Saturday night?

Do you ever do a superb job
of buying groceries for the week
but fail to take home
the one ingredient you can't do without
for tonight's dinner?

You, too?

1

WHETHER REPORT

Just couldn't get moving
to plant those flowers
last week when the sun was bright
and Spring was prematurely
here to stay.

Last night's frost
erased my guilt,
replaced the "lazy" label
with Discerning and Wise.

ASSOCIATIONS

Every time I lift a knife
to score the hot dogs
I think of Marian
who came to our house
during my son's birthday party
and insisted that I score the hot dogs.

Every time I marinate the turkey chunks
to make "chicken salad"
I think of Harriet
who taught me that turkey's best
for making chicken salad.

Every time I pour the cooked spaghetti
and its water into a colander
I think of Jane
who told me that the first time
she cooked spaghetti
she poured the whole potful down the drain.

Makes me wonder
when they think of me....

Rx: SEX

You tell me sex
will cure all ills:
tennis elbow,
a headache,
even the common cold!
Magic medicine for every ailment,
particularly good
for insomnia.

WHY?

Why is it
that some days
whatever I try to do
needs to be preceded
by something else
that has to be done first?

To send a spontaneous note to an old friend
takes three phone calls
to get an address...
To close a packet that's ready to mail
guarantees that the stapler
needs staples...
To put tonight's dinner in the oven
means that first I have to clean
yesterday's soaking casserole!

"—WHATEVER THAT MEANS"

I love you, he said,
whatever that means.
Love to look at you,
be near you,
with you,
close to you all the time,
well, most of the time.

When I'm with you, she said,
I love your glance,
your presence,
your touch
and warmth,
your company.
Well, most of the time
I love you, too,
whatever that means.

THE MENDING BOX

Our mending box is an old pine relic,
an antique sugar bucket,
holding John's sock with a hole,
Tom's shirt missing a button,
a torn sleeve of Dan's,
a hem to change for Eleanor.
Are they there for repair?
Of course not.

Our old bucket just holds
the garments until they're outgrown
and guilt-free-ready
for Goodwill.

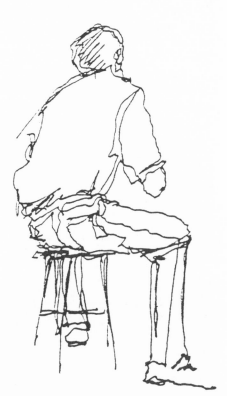

TOTAL SHARING

The only thing I can figure is
he wants to keep no secrets from me,
none at all.
Why else would he leave every hair
and every finger nail shard
in the bathroom bowl?
For me to count?

THE JET-SET FLY

Oh, little fly,
flitting about the cabin,
how did you get aboard this 747?
Did you book the space?
Are you a studied stowaway?
or an accidented passenger?
What brought you to the airport
in the first place?
What chain of events
put you on a flight from New York to Paris?
Oh, jet-set fly,
Parlez-vous Français?

MORNING PERSON

Every day
she's up at six,
thinkwheels spinning
with great ideas,
beautiful dreams,
brilliant plans.

Every day!

But ...
every day by two o'clock
she's ready for a nap.

BRAIN-WASHED AND DRIED

When phone answering machines
were still a novelty
I felt intimidated talking
to Nobody.

Leaving messages now is so routine
that I was startled today
into momentary silence
when a repairman spoke a real
Hello.

MAN'S WORK

When it comes to liberating
a dead morning-mouse
from the midnight-mousetrap,
even a liberated female may opt
for Traditional Roles.

SURVIVAL SKILLS

I know I'm too dependent
on the grocery store.
I have friends and relatives
who bake exotic breads.
If there's a baker's strike,
they'll cope.

I have friends and relatives
who grow organic vegetables,
prepare *gazpacho* and *ratatouille*
from scratch,
and know where to use esoteric herbs.
They freeze corn and can tomatoes,
sprout alfalfa seeds and brew yogurt.
If there's a shortage
on the grocer's shelves,
they'll shop at home.

If there's an earthquake, flood,
blizzard or truck strike,
I'm in trouble.
My survival skills
are limited to comparing prices
of jug wines, ice cream, and chunky
peanut butter.

AN EARLY HUG

Before they get out of bed
they roll toward each other,
just to lie close
and share a tender hug.
His arm around her shoulder
gives her support.
She rests her head
upon his chest.

That gentle embrace
nourishes them to start the day;
and if her forehead should begin
to itch
she can scratch it lightly
on his emery chin.

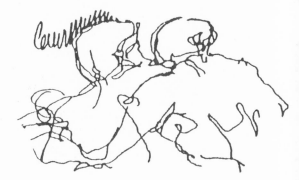

FETISH

I remember it well
because I want to remember it well,
my mother saying,

> I make housekeeping a fetish
> I hope you won't do the same.

Oh, I don't, Mother dear,
indeed I don't.
Neat on the surface,
the house has hidden clutter:
cartons of notes to file or pitch;
boxes of family pictures
waiting to be albumed;
piles of clothes to wash, mend,
put away, or give away.
Then there's the mail!
The mail defeats me.
I don't know where to put it
before and after it's read.

I wish just now and then
I'd be compulsively neat.
I'd like a touch of Mother's fetish
for a little while each day.

VACATIONEER

The day our window-wiper freezes
and the defroster's not melting ice
don't let your card arrive
complaining the sun's too hot
in Puerto Rico.

The day the furnace quits
and we're burning the last of our
firewood
I don't want to hear of sand
between the sheets
in Acapulco.

With snow as high as hubcaps
I'll still meet you at the airport
but please don't wave at me
with your wet bathing suit
in a plastic bag.

Then home, if you like,
keep your sunburn going with
sunlamp and cosmetics,
telling me all the time you're fading.
I'll even admire your fading tan
if you won't scratch mosquito bites
in a room with me.

alas!

the trouble
with those acquaintances
who hold strong opinions
who hold strong opinions
and give unsought
authoritive advice on any
and many subjects
is that sometimes
they're right

PRE-WORD PROCESSOR

Today's a found-and-snowbound day
and what do I do
that's different?
Watch a TV movie
with 47 commercials?
read a book straight through?
wallow in musical sounds?
No, I clean my beloved typewriter:
pick the stuck ink
out of the y's and b's and h's;
then, with damped cloth,
erase the dirty finger marks
from every plastic key,
even the Back-Space and Shift-Lock.
I find my word-machine
every bit as shiny and beautiful
as the hairdos in shampoo commercials.

So now when I begin to write
my every word is squeaky clean.

NOT IN CONCERT

When she attends a concert,
she wants to hear the music.
When he goes, it's a good program
if it puts him to sleep.

She might enjoy a doze sometime,
but can't let herself relax that much;
besides she wants to stay awake
to deliver a sudden nudge
just in case he starts to snore...

COMPANY'S COMING

Slow down, lady.
Relax on your housecleaning.

You work too hard on window-washing,
floor-waxing, rug-scrubbing.
The hostess magnifies peeling paint spots
and scuffed baseboards in her mind,
but guests only notice the company
and conversation,
oh yes, and the food.

But do take a minute to hang guest towels
in the bathroom;
and while you're there
wipe the shelves in the medicine chest
and pitch those ancient prescriptions.

Many guests can't resist taking
a hasty inventory.

GET A BANKCARD

Is your account at this branch?
the teller at the drive-in bank accosts me
with her microphone turned up loud.
I don't know why she asks;
no one has before.
What do you mean?
Do you have an account here?

I sit up tall as I can
and shout at that stellar-teller,
We have a great arrangement at our house;
had it for years:
my husband deposits money downtown
and I tour the branches all week to take it out!
She gives me my cash with a glaring glare.

No lollypop.

A GOOD MORNING

A remarkable day today:
before breakfast
I'd culled out 40 magazines
for the discard heap,
sewed on two buttons,
dressed for the day,
and sudsed the hand laundry.

Now it's just 10 a.m.
I've answered three letters
that have been waiting
for months.
Even my typing's going smoothly
with only a few mistakes.

Most days I fight the internal conflict
of want-to-do, have-to-do,
and reluctance to do anything.

Today I'm energetic, relaxed,
moving easily from task to task.
Today I woke up
free.

yellow tulip

oh yellow tulip
last year you
blossomed
in the bed with
all the other tulips ...
what happened over
the winter?
did the earth
move?
did your bulb
crawl underground?

this Spring you
bloom
in the grass
six inches away from
your siblings...
oh yellow tulip
how did you manage to
fall out of bed?

BUMPER CROP

It's been a great year for tomatoes.
The crop is so plentiful this August
we have far more than we
or our neighbors can use;
so off I go each day with a brown bagfull
to give to friends, colleagues, salespeople,
passersby, anyone who will enjoy.
Well, up to this week I felt like Lady Bountiful,
but now, I fear,
I may be forced to deal with homemade
tomato ketchup, tomato relish,
dilled tomatoes, and barbecue sauce.
Every place I turn today someone else carries
a brown bag just like mine.

Wanna trade?

DROUGHT DILEMMA

Do we admire our friend's
lush green grass
or do we criticize him
for permitting
his water sprinkler
to keep on spinning?

HOMEGROWN VEGGIES

Let's see now,
total harvest for the season?
Parsley, chives, bibb lettuce
plentiful,
one zucch,
four eggplant,
twenty tomatoes.
Flunked broccoli,
but the rest really did taste good
fresh from the garden.
Well, my labor's mostly "for fun"
and I won't charge for new washers
or the extra 25 feet of garden hose;
but
with rototill, fertilizer, city water,
organically approved powdered sprinkles,
a touch of hired help,
maybe it's a blessing
my math is poor
and I can't figure out the cost
per pound.

ECOLOGY/APOLOGY

I kill spiders and ants with an apology:
Outdoors we're friends,
but you shouldn't have come into my house.
Daddy-long-legs (few and far between)
I lift gently by one leg, carry outside,
then release.
Ladybugs and fireflies
I cup in my hands,
then punch open the screen door
with my shoulder to set free.
BUT
mosquitoes and houseflies
on my Evil-Disease-Carrying List
I kill fiercely, ruthlessly,
without a moment's hesitation.

Rachel Carson, please forgive me.

THANKSGIVING GARDEN

It's been a mild Fall:
threats of "the freeze,"
not yet the real thing.
With impatient impatiens gone,
petunias hit-and-missing,
the mums decided this week
to hibernate.
We've harvested the green tomatoes;
still snipping chives and parsley.
Through it all
those magenta snapdragons
keep waving
their valiant heads.

DECEMBER MADNESS

Which of us looks more peculiar?
those foolish daisies
blooming in the snow
or silly me
out there picking them?

after the blizzard

howling winds throughout the night
blow a monstrous mound of snow
our way
then total silence
so quiet we hear it
no carsounds
no airplane noise
no movement at all
on our usually busy street
no people this morning
how still it is
white and beautiful from our window
looking out

A BETTER WHAT?

I saw in a store today a new product,
"Clean-Catch (TM) Mousetrap."
The cardboard and plastic package says,
"Reusable! You never see or touch
the dead mouse."

It's safe with me.
I'll never look at a dead mouse
or touch one
or recycle a newfangled trap either.

Still, there's a societal obligation,
don't you think,
to take formal note
whenever someone claims to have made
a better mousetrap?

COMMON GROUND

THE SOCK CONSPIRACY

Put in six, take out five.
Put in four, take out three.
I thought it would be different
on vacation.
This rented place is like a doll house,
appliances all new and almond colored.
BUT, one problem, I've decided,
must be a chronic condition
of laundry machines everywhere.

Put in two socks, take out one.
The machinery here eats them
too.

superduper

if she bustles
as she walks into the meeting late
and must rush off early
for her next appointment

if she keeps shuffling papers
and writing lists of things to do
and even acts confused at times
with too many scattering thoughts

if she always answers the phone
breathlessly
as if she's just been called away
from an earth-shaking conference

people think she's terribly busy
and terribly important

don't they?

courage

what looks like courage
on the outside
may just be jellied chicken broth
contained in a body suit

READING IN BED

The book must have fallen
out of my hands,
open pages face down,
its spine jack-knifed on the floor.
Lost my place;
the bookmark's flown.
God knows what time it was
when I fell asleep.
I have no memory of it.
Who turned out the light?
Maybe God knows.

hey, you!

please don't tell me
you've gotta read that book/you'll love it
you've gotta see that show/you'll love it
you'll laugh out loud
you'll cry your eyes out

just toss me a title
then I'll tell you
if I laughed out loud
cried my eyes out
loved it
loathed it
or even thought about it

next time
if you're still speaking to me
don't spoil my fun

CEMETERY FLOWERS

Why do you take flowers to the cemetery
on Mothers Day, Fathers Day,
Memorial Day?
I asked the old man,
Why not an ordinary Tuesday
when you're thinking of your mother,
your father, or the others who are there?

I chided his conformity, his adherence
to ritual,
because I believed in free expression.
I was young.
Never do anything routinely,
every day, every week, let alone every year,
I thought in those days.

But now I've learned.
If we don't take flowers to the cemetery
on those special days,
Mothers Day, Fathers Day, Memorial Day,
we don't take the flowers.

PRESCRIPTION FOR MYOPICS

pulling weeds and grass
out of the myrtle bed
is soothing summer therapy
for near-sighted
perfectionists

AT THE AIRPORT

I glimpse them coming down the ramp
but I walk the other way
so I won't see them
and they won't see me.

They're old acquaintances;
I have nothing against them,
but I'm short on energy today,
reluctant to greet or be greeted.

I'm proud of protecting myself,
but a twinge guilty?

Forget it.
They probably glimpsed me too
and feel exactly the same way.

windy city

in Chicago
on Michigan Avenue
her wrap-around skirt
is a run-around
today

SEAT OF THE PROBLEM

Upturned seat,
toilet, that is,
in the middle of the night:
I curse at the cold shock
of sitting on the icy porcelain rim,
the unexpected jolt to my balance.

In the dark I wonder
about that sometimes upturned seat.
In the dark I wonder:
Is it grounds for divorce?

DEATH OF A SMALL DOG

Just a small dog is gone,
a quiet, timid, gentle
member of the family
for over a dozen years.

For so small a dog
the void is surprisingly
large.

OCTOBER ALREADY?

Comes the first frost
and you know you won't pick up
those rust-colored chrysanthemums
you thought of planting...

Comes the first frost
and you know you won't get around
to scrubbing the backyard hammock
so it can dry in the warm sun...
You won't spray-paint those flower pots
or transplant the ivy
or put in new tulip bulbs this season.

You've run out of summer,
a secret relief.
It will all wait for next year's
agenda.

MAJOR MINOR

Minor surgery
is Minor
only
when performed
on Other People

A SIMPLE LITTLE DINNER

Simple dinner tonight, I thought:
only two of us at home
and good left-overs that fit together.

Cleanup should be easy:
two plates,
two wine glasses,
two salad bowls.
Just a few relishes to put away
and the cheese pot we call *hors d'oeuvres*.

I hate cleaning salad bowls.
Get it over fast;
then do the plates and glasses.

A simple little dinner, wasn't it?
How could I use six pots?

a genuine optimist

he must be an optimist
whether he knows it or not
he tastes before seasoning
even
institutional food

QUIZ

What do you know about your mate
really?
Do you know
how the day goes?
how the hours are used?
where the thoughts travel?
what's in the heart?

Have you asked
lately?

BODY SHOP

Although she might like the results
of a tummy-tuck or fanny-lift,
she's not brave enough for elective surgery.
She thinks she doesn't envy women
with porcelain facelifts,
but she'd welcome an over-the-counter potion
for sagging veins and flagging muscles.

What she wants is a Body Store
like the Phone Store.
There she could buy replacement parts
or trade the old rotary dial
with shabby case and tangled cords
for a stylish, musical touch-tone
with a trim and classy chassis.

Maybe a Princess?

confucius might say

when you're in a hurry
to get the conference over
and all those problems solved
temptation is to talk fast
wisdom is to listen fast

UNTIMELY

I used to think untimely death
meant sixteen
or twenty
or thirty.

And then
when I was forty
I upped the number
from forty-two
to fifty-nine.

But now
untimely death has become
anything under ninety-eight.

SMALL REWARD

After a trip
and mail's piled up for weeks,
we pick out bills to pay,
magazines and catalogues
to scan,
invitations to meetings, concerts,
gallery openings.

The ones we want to attend or "hafta"
get listed on the calendar.
The "maybe's" we put aside.

Then weeks later when it's really truly
Pitchin' Day,
what joy it is to throw away notices
of all those events whose dates
have come and gone.

THE WRONG LINE

Everyone nods with empathy
when I complain
that I'm always in the slow line.
At the bank,
or the grocery
and all ticket counters,
when there's a choice
I pick the wrong line.

Now, if everyone has the same problem,
who are those people
in the other line?

READING READINESS

She says she's ready to leave
but goes upstairs for gloves and glasses.
She say's she's ready to go
but stops to look up the address they need.
Then she gets her coat and purse
but takes a minute to repair a smeared finger nail.

He used to go out and start the car
when she first said she was ready;
then he'd wait and wait
and grow angrier and angrier.

Now he sits on the couch with a book
and doesn't put his coat on
till she's standing at the door to the garage.

He finds he gets a lot of reading done.

FLY AWAY

The best gift we give a child
is independence.

But how to do it?
With love and example
and trust in the winds.

We let the kite string out
gingerly,
carefully,
studiously...

and then let go.

head-less wonder

when she's at the desk
she longs to be digging and clipping
in the garden

when she's in the yard
she keeps thinking of letters
she's been meaning to write all week

the day she cleans her closet
is the day that's perfect
for golf

the morning she's on the golf course
she remembers company's coming for dinner
and wishes she'd done the cooking yesterday

the body goes one way
the head another
absent-minded? fragmented? schizy?

would life be a little less hectic
if the heart and head
would get their act together?

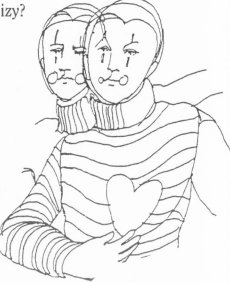

in happy limbo

over the clouds
above the mundane
floating in space
nowhere now
away from shops and menus
telephone and market lists
no need to think of tomorrow
or last week's unfinished business
won't even contemplate unpacking and laundry
and putting away suitcases
still floating serenely
over the clouds
above the mundane
for the moment divorced
from all responsibility

A FINE LINE OF DISTINCTION

The question is not
How well do you know me?
The question is
How well do you want to know me?

FIRST ASSEMBLY

It's the gathering of a new group,
our first meeting today.
The convener calls the members to order.
He asks us at the start to introduce ourselves,
so we go around the large table
slowly announcing our names.
I've always had trouble remembering names
but I want to catch as many as I can.
I listen attentively,
but all the while I'm aware of a small uneasy
bubbling in my head.

As the name-saying comes closer my way
I feel inside me
the merest whisper of that nervous feeling:
when it's my turn
will I know my name?

OFF AND RUNNING

Do you ever simply gather your bundles
and keys to the car,
pull out of the garage and go?
Or are you like me, an athlete-anonymous,
jogging back into the house
once, twice, some days even a third time
to get directions left by the phone?
or the package to return to the store?
possibly even the keys to the car?

Did you say you're going to your aerobics class?
I get all the exercise I can handle
just getting out of the house.

IT'S A GAME?

With your natural swing, they always tell her,
you could really be a good golfer,
if you'd work at it...

Take lessons? Practice?
She'd rather walk on grass, even Rough,
gaze at trees, clouds,
and swing her natural swing.

As a kid she took lessons
from an Authentic Scottish Pro.
She likes hitting a wood-when-it's-good.
Around the greens she knows
she needs to improve her shots, lots.
Sometimes she attends a clinic
or seeks a tip.
Ann gave her a putting lesson.
Carolyn taught her to blast out of sand.
It could be fun to
bring down the handicap,
win a match now and then,
but work at it?

Sure she's mad
on a day with too many slices, shanks,
or balls in the creek.
She may quit that day,
but go back another.
An occasional "Come back tomorrow" drive
keeps her coming back,
though probably not tomorrow.

She might want to work at it,
but...

The Rachel and Ann Nine Hole Group.